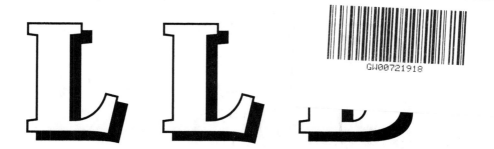

LAND LAW
Suggested Solutions

UNIVERSITY OF LONDON

June Examination 1991

HLT Publications

HLT PUBLICATIONS
200 Greyhound Road, London W14 9RY

Examination Questions © The University of London 1991
Solutions © The HLT Group Ltd 1991

ISBN 1 85352 976 1

British Library Cataloguing-in-Publication.

A CIP Catalogue record for this book is available from the
British Library.

Printed and bound in Great Britain.

Contents

Acknowledgement

The questions used are taken from past University of London LLB (External) Degree examination papers and our thanks are extended to the University of London for the kind permission which has been given to us to use and publish the questions.

Caveat:

The answers given are not approved or sanctioned by the University of London and are entirely our responsibility.

They are not intended as 'Model Answers', but rather as Suggested Solutions.

The answers have two fundamental purposes, namely:

a) To provide a detailed example of a suggested solution to examination questions, and

b) To assist students with their research into the subject and to further their understanding and appreciation of the subject of Laws.

Note:

Please note that the solutions in this book were written in the year of the examination for each paper. They were appropriate solutions at the time of preparation, but students must note that certain caselaw and statutes may subsequently have changed.

Introduction

Why choose HLT publications

Holborn College has earned an International reputation over the past ten years for the outstanding quality of its teaching, Textbooks, Casebooks and Suggested Solutions to past examination papers set by the various examining bodies.

Our expertise is reflected in the outstanding results achieved by our students in the examinations conducted by the University of London, the Law Society, the Council of Legal Education and the Associated Examining Board.

The object of Suggested Solutions

The Suggested Solutions have been prepared by College lecturers experienced in teaching to this specific syllabus and are intended to be an example of a full answer to the problems posed by the examiner.

They are not 'model answers', for at this level there almost certainly is not just one answer to a problem, nor are the answers written to strict examination time limits.

The opportunity has been taken, where appropriate, to develop themes, suggest alternatives and set out additional material to an extent not possible by the examinee in the examination room.

We feel that in writing full opinion answers to the questions that we can assist you with your research into the subject and can further your understanding and appreciation of the law.

Notes on examination technique

Although the SUBSTANCE and SLANT of the answer changes according to the subject-matter of the question, the examining body and syllabus concerned, the TECHNIQUE of answering examination questions does not change.

You will not pass an examination if you do not know the substance of a course. You may pass if you do not know how to go about answering a question although this is doubtful. To do well and to guarantee success, however, it is necessary to learn the technique of answering problems properly. The following is a guide to acquiring that technique.

1 Time

All examinations permit only a limited time for papers to be completed. All papers require you to answer a certain number of questions in that time, and the questions, with some exceptions carry equal marks.

It follows from this that you should never spend a disproportionate amount of time on any question. When you have used up the amount of time allowed for any one question STOP and go on to the next question after an abrupt conclusion, if necessary. If you feel that you are running out of time, then complete your answer in *note form*. A useful way of ensuring that you do not over-run is to write down on a piece of scrap paper the time at which you should be starting each part of the paper. This can be done in the few minutes before the examination begins and it will help you to calm any nerves you may have.

2 Reading the question

It will not be often that you will be able to answer every question on an examination paper. Inevitably, there will be some areas in which you feel better prepared than others. You will prefer to answer the questions which deal with those areas, but you will never know how good the questions are *unless you read the whole examination paper*.

You should spend *at least* 10 MINUTES at the beginning of the examination reading the questions. Preferably, you should read them more than once. As you go through each question, make a brief note on the examination paper of any relevant cases and/or statutes that occur to you even if you think you may not answer that question: you may well be grateful for this note towards the end of the examination when you are tired and your memory begins to fail.

3 Re-reading the answers

Ideally, you should allow time to re-read your answers. This is rarely a pleasant process, but will ensure that you do not make any silly mistakes such as leaving out a 'not' when the negative is vital.

4 The structure of the answer

Almost all examination problems raise more than one legal issue that you are required to deal with. Your answer should:

i) *identify the issues raised by the question*

This is of crucial importance and gives shape to the whole answer. It indicates to the examiner that you appreciate what he is asking you about.

This is at least as important as actually answering the questions of law raised by that issue.

The issues should be identified in the first paragraph of the answer.

ii) *deal with those issues one by one as they arise in the course of the problem*

This, of course, is the substance of the answer and where study and revision pays off.

iii) *if the answer to an issue turns on a provision of a statute, CITE that provision briefly, but do not quote it from any statute you may be permitted to bring into the examination hall*

Having cited the provision, show how it is relevant to the question.

iv) *if there is no statute, or the meaning of the statute has been interpreted by the courts, CITE the relevant cases*

'Citing cases' does not mean writing down the nature of every case that happens to deal with the general topic with which you are concerned and then detailing all the facts you can think of.

You should cite *only* the most relevant cases - there may perhaps only be one. No more facts should be stated than are absolutely essential to establish the relevance of the case. If there is a relevant case, but you cannot remember its name, it is sufficient to refer to it as 'one decided case'.

v) *whenever a statute or case is cited, the title of statute or the name of the case should be underlined*

This makes the examiner's job much easier because he can see at a glance whether the relevant material has been dealt with, and it will make him more disposed in your favour.

vi) *having dealt with the relevant issues, summarise your conclusions in such a way that you answer the question*

A question will often say at the end simply 'Advise A', or B, or C, etc. The advice will usually turn on the individual answers to a number of issues. The point made here is that the final paragraph should pull those individual answers together *and actually give the advice required.* For example, it may begin something like: 'The effect of the answer to the issues raised by this question is that one's advice to A is that ...'

vii) *related to (vi), make sure at the end that you have answered the question*

For example, if the question says 'Advise A', make sure that is what your answer does. If you are required to advise more than one party, make sure that you have dealt with all the parties that you are required to and no more.

5 *Some general points*

You should always try to get the examiner on your side. One method has already been mentioned - the underlining of case names, etc. There are also other ways as well.

Always write as *neatly* as you can. This is more easily done with ink than with a ball-point.

Avoid the use of violently coloured ink eg turquoise; this makes a paper difficult to read.

Space out your answers sensibly: leave a line between paragraphs. You can always get more paper. At the same time, try not to use so much paper that your answer book looks too formidable to mark. This is a question of personal judgment.

NEVER put in irrelevant material simply to show that you are clever. Irrelevance is not a virtue and time spent on it is time lost for other, relevant, answers.

EXAMINATION PAPER

UNIVERSITY OF LONDON
LLB EXAMINATION
PART I
for External Students

LAND LAW

Monday, 3 June 1991: 10.00am to 1.00pm

Answer *four* of the following *eight* questions

1. 'There is no justification today for retaining two methods of creating settlements of land.'

    Discuss. If a single method is to be adopted, what form should it take?

2. In 1980 Peter granted a lease of a house to Thomas for a term of 30 years subject to covenants to pay rent, to keep the house in a good state of repair and not to use the house for business purposes. Performance of the tenant's covenants was guaranteed by a surety, Simon. In 1989 Thomas granted a sublease of the house to Richard for a term of ten years and in 1990 Thomas assigned his lease to Stephen. In 1991 Peter assigned his reversion to Arthur.

    Arthur has received no rent this year, the house is in urgent need of repair and Richard is proposing to start a business in the house.

    What remedies does Arthur have, and against whom?

3. As Ann and Liza were close friends and were doing the same post-graduate course, they decided to share a flat. After looking for a month they found a two-room flat belonging to Lionel which suited them. Lionel insisted on each of them entering into separate but identical 'licence' agreements. Each agreement provided that the licence was to run for nine months from 1 September 1990 and that the licensee agreed to pay £200 per month as licence fee as well as 50% of the outgoings on the flat. The agreement further stated that the licensor should retain a key to the flat and that he reserved the right to occupy

3

the flat whenever he wished. The agreement denied that the licensee was to have exclusive possession of the flat or any part of the flat. Ann and Liza each signed their agreements and entered into possession of the flat on 1 September 1990. Nine months later Lionel told them to leave and, when they refused, he began making abusive telephone calls to them in the middle of the night.

Advise Ann and Liza.

4. In 1980 Mr and Mrs Hall purchased a cottage as their matrimonial home. The price of the cottage was £60,000, of which Mr Hall provided £30,000, Mrs Hall provided £20,000, and Mrs Hall's mother, Norma, provided £10,000 as a wedding gift for the couple. The cottage (the title to which was not registered) was conveyed into Mr Hall's sole name. In 1987 Mr Hall mortgaged the cottage to the Quickfix Bank in order to raise some money to invest in his brother's construction business. Mrs Hall knew about the mortgage, but, when the bank's representative came to inspect the cottage prior to granting the mortgage, she was away on a week's holiday. Recently Mr Hall has started to default on his mortgage payments and the bank is threatening to bring possession proceedings with a view to selling the cottage.

Advise Mrs Hall as to her position. If the cottage was sold, how would the proceeds of sale be distributed?

5. In 1984 John and Karen met and became lovers. At the time they were both married and living with their spouses, but they both hoped to obtain divorces and then to marry each other. In 1985 Karen became pregnant by John and John purchased a flat for her to live in. Karen gave up her job, left her husband and moved into the flat. Shortly afterwards she gave birth to a daughter, Clare. The flat was conveyed into John's sole name and he paid both the deposit on the purchase price, all the bills and all the repayments. For three years John provided Karen with the financial support for herself and Clare. In 1988 Karen found a good job and thereafter supported herself and her daughter as well as spending some money on maintaining and decorating the flat. On one or two occasions Karen asked John why he did not put the flat in their joint names, and he replied that it was because of his tax position, but that she had no reason to worry because she could stay in the flat for as long as she wished and because he was leaving her the flat in his will.

In 1991 John was killed in a car crash. In his will he left his entire estate to his wife, Wilma. His executors now seek possession of the flat with a view to selling it.

Advise Karen.

6. Peter owned a house at No 12 Church Street and Quentin owned the neighbouring house at No 14 Church Street. The titles to both properties were registered under the Land Registration Acts. In 1975 Peter erected a tool-shed partly on his own garden and partly on a strip of the garden of No 14 without Quentin's consent. In 1985 Peter sold No 12 to James who continued to use the shed and in 1990 Quentin sold No 14 to Henry. Henry now wants James to remove the shed.

   Advise James. How would your advice differ if the land was unregistered?

7. 'Once a mortgage always a mortgage and nothing but a mortgage. The meaning of that is that the mortgage shall not make any stipulation which will prevent a mortgagor, who has paid principal, interest, and costs, from getting back his mortgaged property in the condition in which he parted with it.' (per Lord Davey)

   Explain this statement and consider the extent to which it remains true today.

8. Pat was the owner of Blackacre and Whiteacre, two adjoining pieces of land. In 1978 Pat leased Blackacre to his friend Mick for ten years at a rent for the purpose of growing vegetables and Pat covenanted to keep the fence which separated the two properties in a good state of repair. In 1980 Mick asked Pat if he could store his tools in a shed on Whiteacre and Pat agreed. In 1982 Mick asked Pat if he and his friends could play football on Whiteacre on Sundays and Pat agreed. In 1988 Pat died, leaving his entire estate to Rob. Rob has now refused to allow Mick to store his tools or to play football on Whiteacre, and Rob has also refused to repair the boundary fence.

   Advise Mick.

SUGGESTED SOLUTIONS

Question 1

'There is no justification today for retaining two methods of creating settlements of land.'

Discuss. If a single method is to be adopted, what form should it take?

Suggested Solution to Question 1

General comment

Although this is not a difficult question for a reasonably well-prepared student, it is probably one which most students would have been better advised not to attempt. Essay questions are deceptively difficult to answer well in examination conditions and it is all too easy to spend a lot of time and words in saying very little of real significance. Certainly anyone who had not read the Law Commission paper on Trusts of Land should have chosen another question.

Skeleton answer

What was the historical justification for two systems? – Do these reasons apply today? – Main characteristics of the SLA settlement – What are the main problems of the SLA? – Is there still a need to retain the SLA? – Is the trust for sale always appropriate? – What alterations should be made to the trust for sale? – Conclusion: suggest single system based on the trust for sale but with some modifications.

Suggested solution

The reason for the present dual system of creating settlements of land is historical. The original idea behind a settlement under the SLA 1925 (and its predecessors) was to retain land in the family, in circumstances where the life tenant would be residing on the property and would require wide powers of management in order to deal with the settled land to the best advantage of all interested persons. The land was likely to be a large estate. By contrast, the idea behind the trust for sale was to create a mechanism for holding land as an investment pending a sale of the land. Considerable differences remain between the two systems but it is by no means clear whether the existence of these differences justifies the retention of both systems.

The legal estate under an SLA settlement is held by the tenant for life and he will make all the management decisions concerning the property, including the decision whether or not to sell. It is impossible by s106 SLA to interfere with his exercise of these powers in any way. Under a trust for sale the legal estate is held by the trustees and they will make all the management decisions, although they may delegate the powers of leasing and management to the beneficiary. The legislation still gives priority to

11

the SLA so that if no proper advice is taken, it is possible to have an SLA settlement by mistake – this is because if successive interests in land are created, there will be a settlement under the SLA unless an 'immediate binding trust for sale' is created, so that a home-made will which leaves a house to the widow for life and then to the children will create an SLA settlement with its attendant expense and complexity. It seems that a grant of a right of residence for life will also create an SLA settlement: see *Bannister* v *Bannister* (1), *Binions* v *Evans* (2).

The Law Commission identified several problems with the working of the SLA in their report on Trusts of Land. The system is complicated and expensive to administer with the requirement for two documents, a vesting deed and a trust instrument, and the need to take out a special grant of probate when the tenant for life dies. Further problems arise with settlements created accidentally under the SLA as these are bound to be improperly created without the required two documents. Conveyancing difficulties arise if it is not clear whether the settlement is under the SLA or a trust for sale as it is unclear whether the tenant for life of trustees should execute the relevant documents. There may well be a conflict of interest between the personal wishes of the tenant for life and the interests of the other beneficiaries and the latter are in a very weak position with no real right to object to the exercise of his powers by the tenant for life.

The conclusion of the Law Commission was that strict settlement under the SLA be abolished. The recommendation was made on the basis that there was no longer sufficient justification in retaining two parallel systems. The historical reasons for two systems no longer applied and research undertaken by the Commission showed that hardly any new settlements were created under the SLA in any event. The mechanism was cumbersome and expensive and its only advantage was that in some cases it was more appropriate for the tenant for life than the trustees to manage the settled property. The Commission suggested granting an enhanced power of delegation to trustees instead. The old reason for a settlement under the SLA was to keep land in the family and this is easier to achieve with a trust for sale by requiring consents to be obtained before sale.

However the Commission did not simply recommend that the trust for sale become the single possible system for creating trusts of land. The trust for sale is used in settlements with successive interests and when concurrent interests exist. In the latter case the trust for sale is an artificial concept. The Law Commission suggested that the type of co-ownership envisaged in 1925 would have been the situation of land being left to children in a will, when a sale would have resulted. In modern cases of co-ownership the land is purchased for occupation primarily rather than as an investment. The doctrine of conversion which applies to trusts for sale is incomprehensible to non-lawyers.

The recommendation was that the strict settlement and trust for sale should both be replaced by a new single system which would apply to all trusts of land, including bare trusts and concurrent interests. The land would be held by trustees with a power to retain and a power to sell. The doctrine of conversion would not apply. The powers of the trustees would be based on those of the absolute owner. The advantages of the new single system would be that it would remove the complexities inherent in a dual system and many conveyancing difficulties would disappear. In most cases it is more appropriate for the trustees to exercise the powers of management, but there would be improved delegation powers if it was wished that the life tenant should manage the property. The new system would be more in accord with the expectations and understanding of the lay person as it applied to co-ownership.

In conclusion, it is difficult to find any real justification for retaining the two systems of settling land and the scarcity of new SLA settlements in practice seems to confirm this view. The historical reasons for the two systems no longer apply. Therefore in the interests of simplicity a single system is preferable. If a single system is to be adopted, the trust for sale is certainly a more appropriate choice than the strict settlement, which is really of little practical relevance today, but there are significant problems with the trust for sale itself. Therefore a new system based on the trust for sale with certain changes is suggested. The emphasis on the duty to sell and the doctrine of conversion would be abolished and the trustees given power both to retain the land and sell it. This system, as put forward by the Law Commission, would be closer to the layman's understanding of the position.

References
(1) [1948] 2 All ER 133
(2) [1972] Ch 359

Question 2

In 1980 Peter granted a lease of a house to Thomas for a term of 30 years subject to covenants to pay rent, to keep the house in a good state of repair and not to use the house for business purposes. Performance of the tenant's covenants was guaranteed by a surety, Simon. In 1989 Thomas granted a sublease of the house to Richard for a term of ten years and in 1990 Thomas assigned his lease to Stephen. In 1991 Peter assigned his reversion to Arthur.

Arthur has received no rent this year, the house is in urgent need of repair and Richard is proposing to start a business in the house.

What remedies does Arthur have, and against whom?

Suggested Solution to Question 2

General comment
A fairly standard question on the enforceability of leasehold covenants which covered privity of estate and contract and remedies available to the landlord. The well-prepared student should have had no real difficulty in coping with any of the points raised.

Skeleton answer
Has benefit or covenants passed to A? – LPA 1925 s141, privity of estate – No privity between A & R? – Has burden passed to S? – Enforcement procedures against S: for failure to pay rent and other covenants – Is there a forfeiture clause? If not, breach of condition? – s146 procedure – Can A proceed against T? – Does benefit of S's covenant run with freehold?

Suggested solution
There is privity of estate and contract between the original landlord and tenant, both of whom remain liable to each other on the covenants in the lease throughout the term. Thomas, as original tenant, remains liable on the covenants in the lease even after he has assigned the lease to Stephen. Arthur is not the original landlord but the assignee of the reversion and in order to enforce the covenants he must show first that the benefit of the covenants has passed to him. By s141 LPA 1925 the benefit of all covenants 'having reference to the subject-matter' of the lease pass with the reversion to the assignee. Such a covenant is said to touch and concern the land or affect the landlord in his normal capacity as landlord or the tenant in his normal capacity as tenant. The covenants in this question are to pay the rent, to keep the property in good repair and not to use the property for business purposes. All these covenants are classic examples of covenants which touch and concern the land and thus the benefit of the three covenants has passed to Arthur.

Arthur may not bring proceedings for breach of covenant against Richard as although the benefit of the covenant has passed to Arthur there is no privity of estate or contract between him and Richard. Richard is only the sub-tenant. As the user covenant is a negative one, it might be directly enforceable against Richard under the law of restrictive covenants, but insufficient information is given to enable this possibility to be considered further. Whether Richard is in breach of his sub-lease, depends on its terms.

In order to enforce the covenants against Stephen, Arthur must show that the burden of the covenants has passed to Stephen and that there is privity of estate or contract between them. At common law the burden of covenants in the lease which touch and concern the land pass with an assignment of the lease (*Spencers Case* (1)). All three covenants touch and concern the land. There is no privity of contract between Stephen and Arthur as they are not the original parties to the lease but there will be privity of estate provided that the lease and the assignment were both legal and not merely equitable. Thus Arthur may enforce the covenants against Stephen.

Arthur may enforce payment of the rent directly by an action for the money or by seizing Stephen's goods through the procedure of distress. He may also be entitled to bring proceedings for forfeiture. The lease is only subject to forfeiture if the covenants are framed as conditions or there is a forfeiture clause in the lease. It is standard for a lease to contain an express forfeiture clause. If there is a forfeiture clause in the lease, Arthur must first make a formal demand for the rent, unless the lease exempts him from so doing. Stephen may obtain relief from forfeiture if he pays the rent due and any costs incurred by Arthur, provided that it is just and equitable to grant relief. The application for relief must be made within six months of the landlord obtaining judgment. If there is at least six months rent in arrears, Stephen has a statutory right to have the proceedings stayed if he pays the arrears of rent and costs before trial. Forfeiture of the lease will automatically determine the sublease to Richard, although Richard has a right to apply for relief independently.

Arthur may sue for damages for breach of the repairing covenant and for an injunction in respect of the user covenant (although this will be of little benefit as Stephen has not himself committed the breach), but he may be entitled to bring forfeiture proceedings if there is a forfeiture clause in the lease. He must first serve notice under s146 LPA 1925 and the notice must specify the breach, require it to be remedied if possible, and require the tenant to pay compensation, if the landlord requires compensation. Arthur must allow Stephen a reasonable time for compliance and three months would probably be sufficient. Certain breaches are considered incapable of remedy but both these breaches are capable of remedy. Stephen may apply for relief on such terms as the court thinks fit and relief is normally granted if the breaches have been remedied. By taking forfeiture proceedings Arthur may indirectly enforce the user covenant against Richard as if the lease to Stephen is forfeited, the sublease will determine. Richard has his own right to ask for discretionary relief.

The performance of the tenant's covenants was guaranteed by Simon as surety. In *P & A Swift Investments* v *Combined English Stores Group* (2), the House of Lords held that the benefit of a surety covenant could run with the reversion if the surety guaranteed performance of tenants' covenants which themselves touched and concerned the land. Provided that the surety given here was not expressed to be personal (whether given to Peter alone, or in respect of Thomas' personal obligations only) the benefit will pass to Arthur. The remedy against Simon will be in damages only.

References
(1)   (1585) 3 Co Rep 16a
(2)   [1988] 2 All ER 885

Question 3

As Ann and Liza were close friends and were doing the same post-graduate course, they decided to share a flat. After looking for a month they found a two-room flat belonging to Lionel which suited them. Lionel insisted on each of them entering into separate but identical 'licence' agreements. Each agreement provided that the licence was to run for nine months from 1 September 1990 and that the licensee agreed to pay £200 per month as licence fee as well as 50% of the outgoings on the flat. The agreement further stated that the licensor should retain a key to the flat and that he reserved the right to occupy the flat whenever he wished. The agreement denied that the licensee was to have exclusive possession of the flat or any part of the flat. Ann and Liza each signed their agreements and entered into possession of the flat on 1 September 1990. Nine months later Lionel told them to leave and, when they refused, he began making abusive telephone calls to them in the middle of the night.

Advise Ann and Liza.

Suggested Solution to Question 3

General comment
This was a predictable question on the lease/licence distinction with particular reference to sharing arrangements. Students who had actually read the relevant cases would have had a definite advantage in answering the question.

Skeleton answer
Is it a lease or licence? – Importance of distinction re security of tenure – Any remedy for harassment under Protection from Eviction Act 1977? – Is there exclusive possession? – Main cases on sharing agreements: joint tenancy or licence? – Is the term reserving to Lionel the right to occupy a sham? – Are separate obligations to pay fatal to a joint tenancy? – Conclusion: suggest on balance points more towards a lease but emphasise this area of law changing all the time.

Suggested solution
The real issue in this case is whether Ann and Liza are tenants or licensees. If they are tenants they may be entitled to security of tenure under the Rent Acts, whereas if they are licensees, their rights depend on the terms of the licence and they will have no security of tenure as the Rent Acts will not apply. Whether they are licensees or tenants they may have a remedy against Lionel's abusive telephone calls under the Protection from Eviction Act 1977. This Act makes it an offence to harass a residential occupier with the intention of causing him to give up his occupation.

Therefore Ann and Liza may be able to prosecute Lionel under this Act, but this will not help them remain in occupation although it may give them some personal satisfaction.

A lessee must have exclusive possession and if there is no grant of exclusive possession there is no lease, although it is possible to have exclusive possession but still a licence. In *Street* v *Mountford* (1) Lord Templemann said 'Where the only circumstances are that residential accommodation is offered and accepted with exclusive possession for a term at a rent, the result is a tenancy.' The court will construe the agreement made by the parties and if, in substance, the agreement is a lease, it is a lease, no matter that the parties have called it a licence. In *Street* v *Mountford* the agreement was held to create a lease even though it clearly stated that it was only a licence. In this case the crucial question is whether Ann and Liza have been granted exclusive possession and the fact that the agreement calls itself a licence is not decisive.

There have been several recent cases on the difficult issues raised by multiple occupation and sharing agreements. Where there are several occupiers there may be a grant of exclusive possession to them all as joint tenants, or there may be no grant of exclusive possession so that all the occupiers are merely licensees. A third possibility, which does not seem to have been argued in the cases, would be that each occupier has a grant of exclusive possession of his own room with a shared right to use the common parts. In *AG Securities* v *Vaughan* (2) there was a six-roomed flat occupied by four persons. Each occupier signed an individual 'licence' agreement and the amount he paid depended on which room he occupied. There was a fairly high turnover of occupants and when one left, either the remaining occupiers found a replacement or the owners advertised for a replacement. A new occupier had to be acceptable to the owners. It was held by the House of Lords that this arrangement created a series of licences not a lease. It was not possible to say that there had been a grant of exclusive possession to the occupiers together. The occupiers had no right to exclude a new occupier introduced by the owners when one occupier left and this term to allow the introduction of new occupiers was clearly not a sham. The four unities essential for joint tenancy were not present. Different occupiers arrived at different times, paid different amounts and stayed for different periods. The argument that when one occupier left, his agreement was terminated and there was an implied surrender by the others followed by a new grant, was considered 'unreal' by the House of Lords.

This case is different to that of *AG Securities* in many respects. There is a term that Lionel may occupy the flat whenever he wishes, but that may well be a sham here. The flat has only two rooms and it is unlikely that it was ever intended by anyone that Lionel would actually move in. In *Antoniades* v *Villiers* (3) the owner granted a 'licence' to an unmarried couple to occupy a two-roomed flat and purported to reserve the right to go into occupation with the couple or introduce another occupier, but the House of Lords said that there had been a grant of exclusive occupation as this term was never intended to be acted upon and was a sham. It seems that in this case both Ann and Liza would have signed or neither. It does not seem to be material that they are two ladies rather than an unmarried couple. In *Hadjiloucas* v *Crean* (4) two ladies agreed to take a two-roomed flat with kitchen and bathroom. Each signed a separate agreement to pay and to use the flat with one other person and if one agreement was terminated the owner could require another person to move in. A retrial was ordered by the Court of Appeal but Lord Templemann in *AG Securities* clearly thought that this arrangement had created a lease with exclusive possession.

One problem does arise as each has a separate obligation to pay. Joint tenancy requires unity of obligation. In *Antoniades* v *Villiers* there were separate obligations to pay but Lord Templemann still held that there was a joint grant of exclusive possession. He said 'A tenancy remains a tenancy even though the landlord may choose to require each of two joint tenants to agree expressly to pay one-half of the rent.' However in the later case of *Mikeover* v *Brady* (5) the fact that there were separate obligations to pay was regarded as a fatal objection to any finding of joint tenancy. In that case there were two 'licence' agreements which imposed separate obligations to pay, although the agreements did not contain any express power to introduce new occupiers and the occupiers did not have the right to leave early on notice. Although the agreements appeared to grant joint exclusive occupation, the Court of Appeal held that there was no joint tenancy because of the separate obligations to pay.

Again in *Stribling* v *Wickham* (6) there were three separate agreements to use premises on a shared basis. It was held that the court must consider all the circumstances and construe the agreement in the light of the circumstances. Here each occupier was responsible for his own payment only and could terminate his own agreement on 28 days notice without affecting the rights of the others. Occupiers changed from time to time and the agreements were not leases but true licences as there was no grant of exclusive occupation. By contrast in *Nicolaou* v *Pitt* (7) there was held to be a grant of exclusive possession and hence a lease in a sharing agreement. In that case the court considered that there had been no real contemplation of introducing another occupier.

Thus some factors in this case seem to point towards a lease and some towards a licence. Ann and Liza appear to have exclusive possession despite Lionel's retention of a key and the term that allows Lionel to occupy the flat with them seems to be a sham as one cannot imagine that the parties ever intended it should be acted upon. However the existence of two separate obligations to pay points away from a joint tenancy and thus towards a licence. If the court is prepared to construe the two agreements together as in *Antoniades* v *Villiers* it is likely that a lease exists. On balance this situation seems closer to *Antoniades* v *Villiers* than *AG Securities* v *Vaughan* or *Stribling* v *Wickham*. Both the latter cases were situations of a fluctuating number of occupiers when each occupier clearly was independent of each other. Here the two agreements appear to be dependent on each other, there is no provision for one of the occupiers to leave early, and the term allowing Lionel to occupy looks like a sham. Therefore it is suggested that Ann and Liza may well have a tenancy and thus protection under the Rent Acts and security of tenure. This area is one where the law is still changing and subsequent cases may point more firmly towards a lease or towards a licence. Lionel would have been better advised to use the new provisions of the Housing Act to grant a short-hold tenancy with guaranteed recovery of possession at the end of the term. Whether they have a lease or licence, Ann and Liza probably have some remedy against Lionel under the Protection from Eviction Act in respect of his abusive telephone calls.

References

(1)   [1985] 2 WLR 877
(2)   [1988] 3 WLR 1205
(3)   [1988] 3 WLR 1205
(4)   [1987] 3 All ER 1008
(5)   [1989] 3 All ER 618
(6)   [1989] 27 EG 81
(7)   [1989] 21 EG 71

Question 4

In 1980 Mr and Mrs Hall purchased a cottage as their matrimonial home. The price of the cottage was £60,000, of which Mr Hall provided £30,000, Mrs Hall provided £20,000, and Mrs Hall's mother, Norma, provided £10,000 as a wedding gift for the couple. The cottage (the title to which was not registered) was conveyed into Mr Hall's sole name. In 1987 Mr Hall mortgaged the cottage to the Quickfix Bank in order to raise some money to invest in his brother's construction business. Mrs Hall knew about the mortgage, but, when the bank's representative came to inspect the cottage prior to granting the mortgage, she was away on a week's holiday. Recently Mr Hall has started to default on his mortgage payments and the bank is threatening to bring possession proceedings with a view to selling the cottage.

Advise Mrs Hall as to her position. If the cottage was sold, how would the proceeds of sale be distributed?

Suggested Solution to Question 4

General comment

It is to be hoped that not too many students talked about overriding interests here as the question clearly states that title is not registered. Although the problems raised by the issues in the question are well-known, there is often a tendency to overlook unregistered land and the doctrine of notice and concentrate on registered land and overriding interests.

Skeleton answer

Does Mrs Hall have an equitable interest and if so, is it binding on the bank? – Legal title in Mr Hall but presumption of resulting trust applies – Does Norma have an interest or did she intend a gift? – What are the original equitable interests? – Unregistered land, so enforceability depends on notice – *Caunce* v *Caunce, Boland* – What are requirements for purchaser without notice: see *Tizard* – If no notice, bank not bound by Mrs Hall's interest – If bank has notice, does Mrs Hall's consent to mortgage mean that she cannot assert her interest against bank? – How should proceeds of sale be divided?

Suggested solution

Mrs Hall needs to establish whether she has an equitable interest in the cottage and if so, whether her interest is binding on the bank as mortgagees. Mr Hall has the sole legal title as the cottage was conveyed into his name alone. However as Mrs Hall provided part of the purchase price there will be a presumption that the cottage is held on trust for the parties in proportion to their respective contributions. Mr Hall provided one half of the purchase price, Mrs Hall one third and the remaining one sixth came from Mrs Hall's mother. It seems unlikely that Mrs Hall's mother has an equitable interest in the cottage since she provided £10,000 as a wedding gift for the couple and therefore there will not be a trust in her favour. Is Mrs Hall entitled to a one third or some larger share?

It may well be that the intention of the parties was that they would be jointly entitled and that Mrs Hall has a half share in equity. She might argue that the gift from her mother was primarily to her although expressed as a gift to the couple, and thus that her contribution is one half of the purchase price. In any event her contribution is at least £25,000 out of £60,000 and it is suggested that the court is likely to find that the couple are entitled to half shares in equity. Is Mrs Hall's interest binding on the bank? She could have registered a Class F land charge to protect her right of occupation under the Matrimonial Homes Act but it seems that she did not do so, or the bank would not have granted the mortgage. Her equitable interest exists behind a trust and its enforceability depends on the old doctrine of notice. Mrs Hall needs to show that the bank had actual, constructive or imputed notice of her rights.

In *Caunce* v *Caunce* (1) the house was conveyed into the name of the husband alone although the wife was entitled to a half share in equity. Unknown to the wife the husband mortgaged the house to Lloyd's Bank. It was held that the bank took free of the wife's equitable interest as a purchaser for value of a legal estate without notice. This decision was criticised by the House of Lords in *Williams & Glyn's Bank* v *Boland* (2) concerning registered land, when it was held in similar circumstances that the wife had an overriding interest binding on the bank under s70(1)(g) LRA 1925. It is clearly not desirable to have the rights of the parties dependent on whether or not the land is registered. The later decision of *Kingsnorth Finance Trust* v *Tizard* (3) is also relevant. In this case the house was again conveyed into the sole name of the husband, although the wife claimed an equitable interest by virtue of her contribution. The marriage broke down and Mrs Tizard started to sleep at her sister's house on some nights. However she still slept at the matrimonial home on her husband's frequent absences and always went there early in the morning to get the children's breakfasts and ensure they were ready for school. She returned there in the afternoon and prepared the evening meal and went away if her husband came back. She kept most of her clothes there. Mr Tizard applied for the mortgage and arranged that his wife and children would be away when the valuer called to inspect one Sunday afternoon. Although on the application form he had described himself as single, he told the valuer that he was married but separated. The valuer's evidence was that he saw signs of occupation by Mr Tizard and the children but not by anyone else.

It was held that Mrs Tizard's interest was binding on the mortgagee as on the facts it was not a purchaser without notice. Mrs Tizard was still in occupation although she did not always sleep there, but in the case of unregistered land occupation in itself is not decisive. The reference to a separated wife, especially since Mr Tizard had previously said he was single, and the presence of the children should have alerted the valuer to make further enquiries. If the mortgagee carried out a proper inspection and did not find a person in occupation, or any evidence of occupation by that person, the mortgagee would have no notice of the rights of that person. An inspection at a time arranged by the mortgagor was not necessarily enough, but it depended on the circumstances of the case. Here the inspection had not been adequate.

In this case Mrs Hall was away on holiday when the inspection was made. It is not known whether the bank knew that Mr Hall was married, or whether there were any children. In *Kingsnorth* the court considered that the mortgagee should be alert for signs of occupation by other persons but that it was not necessary to open drawers and cupboards. It is suggested that if the bank knew that Mr Hall was married, or should have seen signs of occupation by Mrs Hall on the inspection, or had detected Mr Hall in making contradictory statements, the bank probably had notice of her rights. However if Mr Hall claimed to be single and there were no signs of occupation by anyone else, it may be that the bank can claim to be without notice of the rights of Mrs Hall.

A further problem is that Mrs Hall apparently knew of the mortgage, although she may not have known of its extent. There have been a number of cases where a wife has signed mortgage documents and later claimed that the mortgage was not binding on her. There is no presumption of undue influence between husband and wife. In *Cornish* v *Midland Bank* (4) a wife was held entitled to damages for negligent advice when the bank failed to advise her of the full meaning and effect of a mortgage, but the mortgage itself was not set aside as the bank had not taken an unfair advantage. In *Kingsnorth Trust* v *Bell* (5) the mortgagee could not enforce the mortgage against the wife as her signature was obtained by the husband's misrepresentations. The mortgagee had instructed the husband to obtain his wife's signature and so was liable for any misrepresentations he made. The mortgagee should have insisted the wife had independent legal advice.

This problem is rather different as Mrs Hall has not signed anything. If the bank had no notice of her occupation it will not be bound by her rights, but if it had notice, will Mrs Hall be unable to enforce her rights as she knew of the mortgage? In *Abbey National Building Society* v *Cann* (6) the defendant claimed an equitable interest in a house purchased by C with the aid of a mortgage. The claim in the House of Lords failed on other grounds but the Court of Appeal held that the defendant's claim failed because she knew that C was going to raise part of the purchase price by a mortgage and therefore had impliedly authorised C to grant a charge over the property having priority to her interest. Although she claimed that the mortgage was greater than she had been informed, she could not complain against the mortgagee that C had exceeded his authority since the mortgagee could not be aware of any limitation. The bank could argue here that as Mrs Hall knew of the mortgage, she had authorised Mr Hall to grant the mortgage in priority to her interest and was bound by it. It would be useful to know whether Mrs Hall knew of the extent of the mortgage.

If the house is sold, the mortgage must be discharged. As discussed above it is not clear whether the mortgage is binding on Mrs Hall's share as well as on Mr Hall's share. The balance of the proceeds will be divided between Mr and Mrs Hall. It has been suggested that originally they were jointly entitled in equity. If Mrs Hall had been in full agreement to the mortgage and fully aware of its extent, it is suggested that the balance will be divided equally. If she had been misled by Mr Hall she may be entitled to claim her share of the equity and have the mortgage discharged out of Mr Hall's share alone.

References
(1)   [1969] 1 WLR 286
(2)   [1981] AC 487
(3)   [1986] 1 WLR 783
(4)   [1985] 3 All ER 513
(5)   [1986] 1 WLR 119
(6)   [1990] 2 WLR 832

Question 5

In 1984 John and Karen met and became lovers. At the time they were both married and living with their spouses, but they both hoped to obtain divorces and then to marry each other. In 1985 Karen became pregnant by John and John purchased a flat for her to live in. Karen gave up her job, left her husband and moved into the flat. Shortly afterwards she gave birth to a daughter, Clare. The flat was conveyed into John's sole name and he paid both the deposit on the purchase price, all the bills and all the repayments. For three years John provided Karen with the financial support for herself and Clare. In 1988 Karen found a good job and thereafter supported herself and her daughter as well as spending some money on maintaining and decorating the flat. On one or two occasions Karen asked John why he did not put the flat in their joint names, and he replied that it was because of his tax position, but that she had no reason to worry because she could stay in the flat for as long as she wished and because he was leaving her the flat in his will.

In 1991 John was killed in a car crash. In his will he left his entire estate to his wife, Wilma. His executors now seek possession of the flat with a view to selling it.

Advise Karen.

Suggested Solution to Question 5

General comment

Another topical question on the area of licences and proprietary estoppel which demanded a good knowledge of case law for a satisfactory answer. Students need to be careful with this type of question that they do not spend time setting out their views on how this type of situation should be dealt with and not spending sufficient time on the law as it stands today.

Skeleton answer

Legal title passes to executors and Wilma entitled to estate under will – What claims does Karen have? – Constructive trust: was there an agreement between the parties? – Has Karen acted to her detriment in reliance? – Contractual licence? – Proprietary estoppel: consider *Coombes* v *Smith, re Basham* – Has Karen relied on any promise? – Flexibility of doctrine – Conclusion: looks unpromising but perhaps has a right to stay until daughter is older.

Suggested solution

Legal title in the flat has passed to John's executors and Wilma is entitled to John's estate under his will. Karen must try to establish some claim which will be binding on the executors. There are a number of possible claims. She could argue that she is entitled to some form of equitable proprietary interest in the flat, that she has some form of licence entitling her to remain there and that she is entitled to some remedy under the doctrine of proprietary estoppel. There is no indication that John ever gave her the deeds of the flat and no possibility on the facts as set out in the question of making a claim of a valid donatio mortis causa under *Sen* v *Headley* (1). The various possible claims will be examined in turn.

John had sole legal title to the flat and in order for Karen to claim a property interest in it, she must show that she is entitled under some form of trust and a constructive trust is the most appropriate here. The recent decision of the House of Lords in *Lloyds Bank* v *Rosset* (2) attempted to clarify the law relating to the circumstances in which the court will impose a constructive trust. If there has been an express agreement between the parties, either prior to acquisition or exceptionally at some later date, the court will impose a constructive trust if the party claiming an equitable interest has acted to his detriment or changed his position in reliance on that agreement. If there has been no such agreement, the court relies on conduct to infer the existence of a common intention to share and Lord Bridge doubted whether anything other than a direct contribution to the purchase price would be sufficient to justify the inference. There does not seem to be any express agreement between the parties prior to the acquisition that it would be shared beneficially and Karen has not made any direct contribution to the purchase price, either initially or by contributing to the mortgage repayments. The work which she did in decorating the flat would surely be disregarded as in *Rosset* itself and *Burns* v *Burns* (3).

There is some evidence that at a later stage, John led Karen to believe that she would have a share in the flat as he said to her that he did not put the flat into joint names because of his tax position. This sounds like *Eves* v *Eves* (4) where the man said that the only reason the property was being put in his name alone was that his female partner was under 21, and *Grant* v *Edwards* (5), where the man told his female partner that the only reason the property was not being acquired in joint names was her divorce proceedings. Both ladies acted to their detriment in reliance on this promise and a constructive trust was imposed in their favour. The difficulty for Karen is that John's statement to her was made sometime after the actual acquisition, but Lord Bridge did indicate that in exceptional circumstances a later agreement might be sufficient. He did not give any guidance as to what would constitute exceptional circumstances were. In any event, has Karen acted to her detriment or changed her position in reliance? She has merely continued to live in the flat, although she might argue as in *Greasely* v *Cooke* (6) that she forewent opportunities of moving elsewhere. This does not sound convincing as the period is not so long that it would now be impossible for her to find other accommodation and she has not foregone employment opportunities as in *Greasely* v *Cooke*. She has spent her own money in maintaining and decorating the flat. This might possibly count as acting to her detriment, if done after John's statement to her, but it could be argued that she did this simply in order to be more comfortable. The more money she spent, the more convincing the argument will sound.

On the whole, a claim based on constructive trust to a share in the property does not look very strong. Karen could claim to have a licence to remain in the flat, but the disadvantage of this claim is that it can only give her a right to remain as opposed to a right in the property itself. In

Coombes v *Smith* (7) the facts were quite similar. The plaintiff claimed a contractual licence on the basis that the defendant had offered to provide a roof over her head if she moved in with him. It was held that there was no enforceable contract. A more attractive claim is one based on proprietary estoppel. Has Karen acted to her detriment in reliance on a mistaken belief in her legal rights? In *Coombes* v *Smith* it was held that the plaintiff had not had a mistaken belief in her legal rights, even though she probably had believed that the defendant would always provide for her. Whenever she had asked for the house to be put into joint names, the defendant had refused and there was no evidence of any discussions about what would happen if the relationship broke down. Karen's case is stronger as John had assured her that she could stay in the flat as long as she wished and that he had left her the flat in his will. It was held in *re Basham* (8) that proprietary estoppel includes cases where the plaintiff is led to believe that he will have a right in the future.

It is still necessary for Karen to show that she acted to her detriment or altered her position on the faith of her belief. In *Coombes* v *Smith* it was held that having a child, moving away from her husband, redecorating and not trying to provide otherwise for herself did not show acting to one's detriment. The actions were either due simply to a desire to live with the defendant, or done as occupier of the property. By contrast, in *re Basham*, a long history of working without pay, foregoing opportunities to move, caring for the deceased and spending her own money to resolve a boundary dispute were sufficient for a claim based on proprietary estoppel when coupled with frequent promises by the deceased that his property would pass to the plaintiff on his death. Karen's situation looks closer to that in *Coombes* v *Smith*. Although John did promise to leave her the flat in his will, it is difficult to see that Karen has changed her position in reliance on that.

In conclusion therefore Karen could try to claim an interest under a constructive trust or base a claim on proprietary estoppel. The difficulty with the trust claim is that she made no contribution to the acquisition and the only evidence of a common intention that there would be sharing is John's statement made after the purchase. Even if that is enough, Karen must still show that she significantly changed her position as a result and she seems merely to have continued as before. There is no real evidence of contract to found a claim based on contractual licence and the remaining possibility is that of proprietary estoppel. Again Karen's difficulty is that although she was mistaken about her future legal rights, it is not easy to see that she acted to her detriment in reliance. Such acts as looking after a child, failing to provide for herself otherwise and redecorating were held insufficient in *Coombes* v *Smith*. However Karen's claim is not hopeless. In *Coombes* v *Smith* the defendant had already conceded that the plaintiff could stay in the house until the child was 17 and that he would pay the mortgage for that period. It might be that the court would use the flexibility of the doctrine of proprietary estoppel to grant Karen some lesser remedy than a transfer of or share in the flat itself and allow her to remain living there for a limited time until her daughter Clare is, say, 17. There was a clear promise made to her and it is a matter of how flexible the court will be about what constituted acting in reliance on that promise.

References

(1)   [1990] 2 WLR 620
(2)   [1990] 2 WLR 867
(3)   [1984] 1 All ER 244
(4)   [1975] 1 WLR 1338
(5)   [1986] 3 WLR 114
(6)   [1980] 3 All ER 710
(7)   [1986] 1 WLR 808
(8)   [1986] 1 WLR 1498

Question 6

Peter owned a house at No 12 Church Street and Quentin owned the neighbouring house at No 14 Church Street. The titles to both properties were registered under the Land Registration Acts. In 1975 Peter erected a tool-shed partly on his own garden and partly on a strip of the garden of No 14 without Quentin's consent. In 1985 Peter sold No 12 to James who continued to use the shed and in 1990 Quentin sold No 14 to Henry. Henry now wants James to remove the shed.

Advise James. How would your advice differ if the land was unregistered?

Suggested Solution to Question 6

General comment
This was probably not a very welcome question to many students as adverse possession is an area of the syllabus which is often omitted in revision and the rules on rectification of the register are sometimes glossed over by those who regard registered land as being solely about overriding interests and in particular s70(1)(g) of the Land Registration Act 1925.

Skeleton answer
Time period for adverse possession – Aggregation of periods of adverse possession by different owners? – Does the register provide a guarantee of title – Squatters rights or overriding interests? – Compensation for rectification? No loss due to overriding interests not rectification – Position on unregistered land.

Suggested solution
The Limitation Act 1980 sets a 12 year period for the recovery of land and the issue in this case is to establish whether Henry may still recover possession of the part of his garden on which the tool-shed has been erected, or whether his right of action has been barred by lapse of time since it is more than 12 years since the tool-shed was erected.

The tool-shed was erected on the garden of No 14 in 1975 and time begins to run as soon as the rightful owner has been dispossessed. Adverse possession is a matter of fact, but in this case it seems clear that Peter's acts are inconsistent with Quentin's ownership. Peter had not established title against Quentin when he sold No 12 in 1985, as only ten years had passed, but it is well-established that the period taking the squatter's interest can add the squatter's period of possession to his own. Thus James may aggregate his own and Peter's periods of occupation. There are various situations in which a longer period of occupation is required or when the date from which time begins to run is postponed but there seems no indication that any of these apply in this case.

When he bought No 14 Henry was registered with freehold absolute and the register will show him as the proprietor of the garden including the part with the tool-shed on it. The register is said to provide a state guarantee of title. However this state guarantee is not comprehensive and if James can show that he has acquired title under the Limitation Act, he will be entitled to have the register rectified under s82 Land Registration Act 1925. When Henry purchased No 14 in 1990 he purchased subject to any overriding interests, and rights acquired or in the course of being acquired under the Limitation Acts are overriding interests under s70(1)(f) LRA 1925. Once title has been acquired by adverse possession the registered proprietor holds on trust for the squatter. James may apply for registration as proprietor and will be registered with an absolute or possessory title as appropriate. His estate is a new one and not a transfer of an existing one and will be treated as a first registration.

Although the LRA 1925 does provide for compensation to be paid to any person suffering loss by reason of rectification of the register under s83, it seems that Henry will not be entitled to compensation here. In *re Chowood* (1) C was registered as proprietor with title absolute to land, but previously L had acquired title to part of that land by adverse possession. The register was rectified against C and C was held not entitled to compensation because C had always bought subject to any overriding interests and C's loss was due not to the rectification but to failing to ascertain the existence of the overriding interest before he purchased. In this case Henry's loss is not due to the rectification but to paying Quentin for land to which Quentin could not make title.

If this were unregistered land James would still be able to claim title by adverse possession but there will be no transfer of title to James from Henry. James's title depends on his possession and the title of Henry is automatically extinguished under s17 Limitation Act 1980.

Reference
(1)   [1933] Ch 574

Question 7

'Once a mortgage always a mortgage and nothing but a mortgage. The meaning of that is that the mortgage shall not make any stipulation which will prevent a mortgagor, who has paid principal, interest, and costs, from getting back his mortgaged property in the condition in which he parted with it.' (per Lord Davey)

Explain this statement and consider the extent to which it remains true today.

Suggested Solution to Question 7

General comment

Most students were probably relieved to find this question on mortgages rather than a problem on priority of mortgages and students with a reasonable knowledge of the relevant case law should have had no difficulty in dealing adequately with this question.

Skeleton answer

Quotation from *Noakes* v *Rice*: facts – Basic principle: once mortgage paid off, mortgagor should be in same position as before the mortgage – *Bradley* v *Carritt* – Contrast *Kreglinger*: why was the collateral stipulation held binding? – Importance of freedom of contract, don't willingly interfere in businessmen's arrangements – Must be independent bargain – Collateral advantage must not be harsh or unconscionable.

Suggested solution

The quotation is taken from the case of *Noakes* v *Rice* (1) and the issue raised is that of the validity of collateral advantages in mortgages. The mortgagee may wish to secure some collateral benefit to himself during the mortgage and even wish to secure the continuance of that benefit after the mortgage debt itself has been paid off. The traditional approach of the courts has been to hold that collateral benefits may not continue after redemption of the mortgage, but that approach has been to some extent modified in order to conform to modern business requirements.

In *Noakes* v *Rice* itself, the mortgage included a covenant that the mortgagor would only purchase liquor from the mortgagee and this obligation was expressed to endure even after the redemption of the mortgage. The mortgagor claimed to be able to pay off the mortgage and be free of the covenant and it was held that he should be able to do so. The House of Lords held that whilst a mortgage may provide for a collateral advantage, provided that the collateral advantage was not oppressive or unconscionable and did not clog or fetter the equity of redemption, the collateral advantage must come to an end when the loan was paid off. It was said that a mortgage must not be converted into something else and since the collateral stipulation is part of the mortgage transaction, it must necessarily end with the mortgage. The mortgagor had mortgaged a free house and was entitled to recover a free house and not a tied house when he had repaid the mortgage.

The same principle can be seen in the slightly later decision of *Bradley* v *Carritt* (2). In that case the mortgagor mortgaged his shares which gave him a controlling interest in the company and the mortgage provided that the mortgagor would use his best endeavours to appoint the mortgagee as the company's broker and would pay him the commission the mortgagee would have earned as broker, were he not actually appointed as broker. Some time after the mortgage had been paid off, the shares were sold and the mortgagee lost his appointment as broker. He then sued the mortgagor for his lost commission. It was held that he could not do so as the stipulation was void. It amounted to a clog on the equity of redemption. If it had been valid, it would have been difficult for the mortgagor ever to have sold his shares without rendering himself liable for it was only if he retained his controlling interest in the company that he could ensure that the mortgagee was appointed as broker.

The leading case in which a collateral stipulation was held to remain binding after redemption is *Kreglinger* v *New Patagonia Meat Co* (3). The loan was made on terms that the mortgagee would not call in the principal for five years provided that all interest payments were made on time, but the mortgagor was free to repay within the five years if he wished. The loan was secured by a floating charge and it was provided that the mortgagor would only sell its sheepskins to the mortgagee for a five year period, although the mortgagee agreed to pay the market price for the sheepskins. The loan was repaid within the five year period and the mortgagor claimed to be able to sell its sheepskins to persons other than the mortgagee. It was held that the term was still binding. The House of Lords held that the granting of the collateral advantage was a separate contract independent of the mortgage contract and since it did not amount to a clog on the equity of redemption, it remained valid after the mortgage itself was paid off.

It was true that the mortgagor was still restricted in the conduct of its business after the mortgage was at an end, but the House of Lords was clearly unwilling to intervene in a transaction freely contracted by businessmen, when there had been no inequality of bargaining power and no oppression of the mortgagee. One difference between the *Kreglinger* case and *Bradley* v *Carritt* and *Noakes* v *Rice* is that in *Kreglinger* the collateral advantage was only to last five years from the making of the mortgage. In *Bradley* v *Carritt*, had the collateral advantage remained valid the mortgagor would have been permanently unable to sell his shares, and in *Noakes* v *Rice* the 'tying' was intended to remain effective throughout the duration of the lease of the premises.

Thus broadly Lord Davey's statement remains true but if there is a stipulation in the mortgage which is independent of it, that stipulation may remain binding on the mortgagor after he has repaid the mortgage, even if it does affect the way he may deal with the mortgaged property. There is no doubt that the courts will be less willing to regard such collateral advantages as independent of the mortgage if there is a personal loan than if there is a business transaction between parties of equal bargaining power. The *Kreglinger* doctrine allows the courts a measure of flexibility and perhaps reflects the fact that the mortgagor is not necessarily now the traditional oppressed figure of the last century.

References
(1)   [1902] AC 24
(2)   [1903] AC 253
(3)   [1914] AC 25

Question 8

Pat was the owner of Blackacre and Whiteacre, two adjoining pieces of land. In 1978 Pat leased Blackacre to his friend Mick for ten years at a rent for the purpose of growing vegetables and Pat covenanted to keep the fence which separated the two properties in a good state of repair. In 1980 Mick asked Pat if he could store his tools in a shed on Whiteacre and Pat agreed. In 1982 Mick asked Pat if he and his friends could play football on Whiteacre on Sundays and Pat agreed. In 1988 Pat died, leaving his entire estate to Rob. Rob has now refused to allow Mick to store his tools or to play football on Whiteacre, and Rob has also refused to repair the boundary fence.

Advise Mick.

Suggested Solution to Question 8

General comment
Another fairly standard question on easements which should have caused no problems to most students with a reasonable grasp of the subject. The areas covered included rights capable of existing as easements and acquisition of easements by implied grant.

Skeleton answer
Does Mick have rights against Rob? – Are storage and the right to play football possible easements? – Four main characteristics of easements – Storage must not amount to exclusive possession – Playing football does not seem to accommodate use of dominant tenement – If rights can be easements, have they been acquired as such – LPA 1925 s62 requirements – Fencing: covenant in lease – Binding on Rob due to s142 LPA and privity of estate – Conclusion: probably Mick can use shed, have fence repaired but not play football.

Suggested solution
If Mick has a legal right to store his tools and play football on Whiteacre, he will be able to enforce his rights against Rob. If these privileges were merely enjoyed by permission of Pat, Rob will not be bound by them.

Mick will need to show that these rights are capable of existing as easements and that he has acquired them as legal easements. There are four essentials of an easement. There must be a dominant and servient tenement, the easement must accommodate the dominant tenement, the dominant and servient tenements must not be both owned and occupied by the same person and the easement must be capable of forming the subject-matter of a grant. The right of storage was recognised as an easement in *Wright* v *MacAdam* (1), but it is clear from the decisions in *Copeland* v *Greenhalf* (2) and *Grigsby* v *Melville* (3) that if the right claimed is so extensive as to amount to exclusive or joint user of the servient tenement it cannot exist as an easement. It seems that this is a question of degree and further information should be sought on the extent of the right claimed by Mick. It seems unlikely that the right he claims could amount to exclusive or joint user of the shed as he is only storing his tools there, but it may depend on the size of the shed and the number of his tools.

The right to play football is not one of the recognised types of easement. There is a dominant and servient tenement and both are not owned and occupied by the same person. Does the 'easement' accommodate the dominant tenement? In *Hill* v *Tupper* (4) a right to put boats on a canal was not recognised as an easement on the ground that the right was not beneficial to the land itself but merely to Hill's business which he conducted on the land. The right was a personal licence. On the other hand in *re Ellenborough Park* (5) it was held that a right to enjoy a park as a communal garden did accommodate the neighbouring houses. In this case Mick grows vegetables on Blackacre and it is difficult to see that the right to play football on Whiteacre accommodates the use of Blackacre for growing vegetables. If this is wrong it is necessary to consider whether the right is capable of forming the subject-matter of a grant. The nature and extent of the right claimed must be capable of exact description. Again in *re Ellenborough Park* a right to wander at large over the servient tenement was considered sufficiently precise. The list of easements is not closed, but a new category of easement must conform to the four essential characteristics. A new easement is unlikely to be recognised if it would require expenditure by the servient owner, or if it is negative in character – *Phipps* v *Pears* (6). This right does not require expenditure and is not negative, nor does it amount to a claim to joint or exclusive user of Whiteacre. However it is suggested that on balance the right to play football would not be accepted as an easement in this case.

Even if these rights, or some of them, are capable of existing as easements, Mick can only enforce them against Rob, if he has acquired them as legal easements. If the 1988 lease to Mick included an express grant of these rights then the terms of the lease (providing it is a legal and not an equitable lease) will be binding on Rob. If there has been no express grant, Mick will need to rely on implied grant. The right to have the fence kept in repair was contained in the original 1978 lease and may have been repeated in the new lease. Provided that the covenant to keep the fence in good repair was contained in the 1988, as well as in the 1978, lease, Mick as tenant can enforce the covenant against Rob as the assignee of the reversion. There is privity of estate between the parties and the burden of the covenant passes to Rob by LPA 1925 s142 since it has reference to the subject matter of the lease

The other two rights were originally enjoyed by permission only and there is no indication that an express grant was made. It is provided in s62

LPA 1925 that, subject to a contrary intent being expressed, every conveyance of land passes with it 'all liberties, privileges, easements, rights, and advantages whatsoever ... enjoyed with the land'. This section has been held to create easements out of rights previously enjoyed by permission. In *Goldberg* v *Edwards* (7), a right of way enjoyed by revocable licence was turned into an easement by a subsequent grant of a lease. There must be diversity of ownership or occupation for s62 to operate – *Long* v *Gowlett* (8). In this case Mick enjoyed the right to store his tools and play football by permission before the new lease was granted and unless a contrary intention was expressed in the new lease, these rights may have been transformed into easements by s62. However s62 will not apply if the rights claimed cannot exist as easements and if the right to play football cannot exist as an easement at all, it will not become one by virtue of s62.

Thus if these rights can exist as easements and have been acquired as such by Mick either by express or implied grant, Mick may enforce them against Rob. If the right to play football is not an easement, it will be a licence and on these facts it will be a bare licence. The licence will not be binding on Rob. If the right of storage is not an easement, it might be either a lease or a licence. In order to be a lease, there must be exclusive possession, which seems unlikely and there does not seem to be a certain term agreed, nor is it a periodic tenancy as no rent is payable. It is more likely that this right, if not an easement, is a licence and not binding on Rob. It seems likely that the covenant to keep the fence in good repair is part of the lease itself and it will then be binding on Rob.

References
(1)   [1949] 2 KB 744
(2)   [1952] Ch 488
(3)   [1974] 1 WLR 80
(4)   (1863) 2 H & C 121
(5)   [1956] Ch 131
(6)   [1965] 1 QB 76
(7)   [1950] Ch 247
(8)   [1923] 2 Ch 177

DETAILS FOR DESPATCH OF PUBLICATIONS

Please insert your full name below

Please insert below the style in which you would like the correspondence from the Publisher addressed to you

TITLE Mr, Miss etc.   INITIALS   SURNAME/FAMILY NAME

Address to which study material is to be sent (please ensure someone will be present to accept delivery of your Publications).

POSTAGE & PACKING

You are welcome to purchase study material from the Publisher at 200 Greyhound Road, London W14 9RY, during normal working hours.

If you wish to order by post this may be done direct from the Publisher. Postal charges are as follows:

UK   - Orders over £30: no charge. Orders below £30: £2.50. Single paper (last exam only): 50p
OVERSEAS   - See table below

The Publisher cannot accept responsibility in respect of postal delays or losses in the postal systems.

DESPATCH All cheques must be cleared before material is despatched.

SUMMARY OF ORDER   Date of order:

				£
			Cost of publications ordered:	
			UNITED KINGDOM:	
OVERSEAS:	TEXTS		Suggested Solutions (Last exam only)	
	One	Each Extra		
Eire	£4.00	£0.60	£1.00	
European Community	£9.00	£1.00	£1.00	
East Europe & North America	£10.50	£1.00	£1.00	
South East Asia	£12.00	£2.00	£1.50	
Australia/New Zealand	£13.50	£4.00	£1.50	
Other Countries (Africa, India etc)	£13.00	£3.00	£1.50	
			Total cost of order:	

Please ensure that you enclose a cheque or draft payable to **THE HLT GROUP LTD for the above** amount, or charge to ❑ **Access** ❑ **Visa** ❑ **American Express**

Card Number

Expiry Date .... Signature ....

ORDER FORM

LLB PUBLICATIONS	TEXTBOOKS Cost £	£	CASEBOOKS Cost £	£	REVISION WORKBOOKS Cost £	£	SUG. SOL. 1985/90 Cost £	£	SUG. SOL. 1991 Cost £	£
Administrative Law	17.95		18.95				9.95		3.00	
Commercial Law Vol I	18.95		18.95				9.95		3.00	
Commercial Law Vol II	17.95		18.95		9.95		9.95		3.00	
Company Law	18.95		18.95		9.95		9.95		3.00	
Conflict of Laws	16.95		17.95							
Constitutional Law	14.95		16.95		9.95		9.95		3.00	
Contract Law	14.95		16.95		9.95		9.95		3.00	
Conveyancing	17.95		16.95							
Criminal Law	14.95		17.95		9.95		9.95		3.00	
Criminology	16.95						+3.00		3.00	
English Legal System	14.95		12.95				*7.95		3.00	
Equity and Trusts	14.95		16.95		9.95		9.95		3.00	
European Community Law	17.95		18.95		9.95		+3.00		3.00	
Evidence	17.95		17.95		9.95		9.95		3.00	
Family Law	17.95		18.95		9.95		9.95		3.00	
Jurisprudence	14.95				9.95		9.95		3.00	
Labour Law	15.95									
Land Law	14.95		16.95		9.95		9.95		3.00	
Public International Law	18.95		17.95		9.95		9.95		3.00	
Revenue Law	17.95		18.95		9.95		9.95		3.00	
Roman Law	14.95									
Succession	17.95		17.95		9.95		9.95		3.00	
Tort	14.95		16.95		9.95		9.95		3.00	

BAR PUBLICATIONS										
Conflict of Laws	16.95		17.95				†7.95		3.95	
European Community Law & Human Rights	17.95		18.95				†7.95		3.95	
Evidence	17.95		17.95				14.95		3.95	
Family Law	17.95		18.95				14.95		3.95	
General Paper I	19.95		16.95				14.95		3.95	
General Paper II	19.95		16.95				14.95		3.95	
Law of International Trade	17.95		16.95				14.95		3.95	
Practical Conveyancing	17.95		16.95				14.95		3.95	
Procedure	19.95		16.95				14.95		3.95	
Revenue Law	17.95		18.95				14.95		3.95	
Sale of Goods and Credit	17.95		17.95				14.95		3.95	

* 1987–1990 papers only
† 1988–1990 papers only
+ 1990 paper only

HLT PUBLICATIONS

All HLT Publications have two important qualities. First, they are written by specialists, all of whom have direct practical experience of teaching the syllabus. Second, all Textbooks are reviewed and updated each year to reflect new developments and changing trends. They are used widely by students at polytechnics and colleges throughout the United Kingdom and overseas.

A comprehensive range of titles is covered by the following classifications.

- **TEXTBOOKS**
- **CASEBOOKS**
- **SUGGESTED SOLUTIONS**
- **REVISION WORKBOOKS**

The books listed above should be available from your local bookshop. In case of difficulty, however, they can be obtained direct from the publisher using this order form. Telephone, Fax or Telex orders will also be accepted. Quote your Access, Visa or American Express card numbers for priority orders. To order direct from publisher please enter cost of titles you require, fill in despatch details overleaf and send it with your remittance to The HLT Group Ltd.